Gorillas
HUGE AND GENTLE

by Caroline E. Walsh

Perfection Learning®

For Mama, who encouraged me from the start.

For Amanda, who loves these creatures as much as possible.

For Emily, who sat patiently on my lap as I typed.

And for Eric, who made this and
everything else in life seem so fun and so wonderful.

And to Margo, thank you for making it all possible.

About the Author

Caroline Walsh was born on December 17, 1964, in Bryn Mawr, Pennsylvania. She graduated from Harvard College and went on to get a master's degree in English from the University of California, Irvine. She has taught English literature and composition to middle- and upper-school students for seven years while living in Rhode Island and California. Her love for gorillas has always been around, but it is her sister's devotion to them that inspired this book.

She presently lives in New Hampshire with her husband Eric and their daughter Emily. When she is not writing, she and her family love to ski, bicycle, sled, and take advantage of all the other fun activities that New England has to offer.

Illustrations: Michele Ackerman, Mike Aspengren, Kay Ewald

Photo Credits: Karl Ammann/Corbis p.12; Yann Arthus-Bertrand/ Corbis pp. 40, 46; D. Franz/Corbis pp. 37, 51; Library of Congress p. 18; Reuters/ Corbis-Bettmann p. 26; UPI/Corbis-Bettmann pp. 16, 19; Kennan Ward/ Corbis p. 43.

© 2016 by Perfection Learning®
Please visit our Web site at:
www.perfectionlearning.com

When ordering this book, please specify:
Softcover: ISBN 978-0-7891-2146-2 or **4991801**
Hardcover: ISBN 978-0-7807-6782-9 or **4991802**
eBook: ISBN 978-1-61384-869-2 or **49918D**

8   9   10   11   12   13   BRP   21 20 19 18 17 16

Printed in the United States of America

Table of Contents

Chapter 1. Gorilla on the Loose 4

Chapter 2. Koko 14

Chapter 3. Wild Gorillas 30

Chapter 4. Murder in the Mountains 39

Chapter 5. Save the Gorilla 49

For More Information 55

Index 56

Chapter 1

Gorilla on the Loose

Silas burst through the door. He was breathless. And he looked scared!

The three other eighth graders in the classroom stared. They had never seen Silas like this. He was never scared.

"Haven't you guys heard?" Silas choked between breaths. "Don't you guys know what's going on?

"A gorilla," he stammered. "A gorilla has escaped from the zoo. I heard it on the news."

Samuel Taylor Middle School was just around the corner from the Smith Park Zoo. Silas passed the zoo every day on his way to school.

"By now, the beast is probably in the building," Silas continued. "Those things are killers! They can eat a human being in one bite. Didn't you see *King Kong*? We're gonna die. If he doesn't eat us, he'll kill us!"

4

Three pairs of wide eyes stared at Silas. They were all too scared to say anything.

"I heard that one gorilla destroyed an entire village in Africa. He ate all the children. He killed their parents. And then he grabbed some of the other people to take home with him. He even squished some!" Silas blabbered.

Whenever Silas spoke, he usually had something gross to say. He knew more gory details about life than anyone else.

A strange sound behind Silas startled all of them. Something or someone was at the door.

Silas backed away slowly. "Hey," Silas tried to whisper, but nothing came out. He tried again. This time there was only a squeak.

Janey filled in. "What if he's out there! What if the gorilla is right outside our door!"

The three sets of eyes that had been on Silas now stared at the door. Each of the eighth graders watched in absolute terror.

The doorknob began to rotate. No one made a sound. No one made a move. No one dared to think about what might happen.

The door flung open. There stood Mrs. Lam.

"What's wrong with all of you?" she asked. "I've never seen you this quiet in the morning. And you all look like you just saw a ghost!"

For a few moments, no one spoke. Janey was the first to break the silence.

"Haven't you heard?" Janey asked. "Silas just told us that a mean gorilla has escaped from the Smith Park Zoo. He could kill us!"

"And by now, he could be in the school building!" Silas gasped. "What are we going to do?"

"We're not going to do anything," Mrs. Lam said. "First of all, the gorilla has been caught. But even if he hadn't been—"

The principal's voice came over the loudspeaker. "Some of you may have heard that a gorilla escaped from the Smith Park Zoo this morning. I want you to know that he has been returned to the zoo. Everything is fine. Please do not be afraid. Our school is completely safe. I repeat, everything is fine. Have a good day. Thank you."

The children in Room 114 did not move. They just stared at their crazy teacher. Why was she so calm? Didn't she know how much danger they had been in?

"I think we need to have a talk about what just happened," Mrs. Lam began. "Why did you all panic when you heard Silas's news?"

"Because gorillas are mean. They eat people," Silas exclaimed. The others nodded their heads in agreement.

"Just a moment," said Mrs. Lam. "Let's think about this some more. The only time most of us ever see gorillas, they're in cages. I think everyone was scared because gorillas are big. And because we don't know very much about them! Not knowing makes us all scared!"

"I don't know much about ladybugs, and they don't scare me!" Silas claimed.

"Give it a rest, Silas!" Janey snapped.

Mrs. Lam continued. "But imagine if we all treated each other that way. I like to get to know my students before I begin to make judgments. And I like to think the same goes for you. You wanted to get to know me before you decided what kind of a teacher I would be.

"So maybe before we accuse gorillas of eating people, we might want to learn more about them." Mrs. Lam went on. "The other day I read something that made me want to know so much more about gorillas. Does anyone know what I'm talking about?"

Janey raised her hand.

Silas rolled his eyes.

"Yes, Janey," Mrs. Lam said.

"Well, I think I may know. My mother showed me some pictures in a magazine of a gorilla holding a little boy."

"What's so great about that?" Silas demanded.

"Just a second, Silas. Let's let Janey finish."

"Well, actually Maddie and I both saw the pictures," Janey said, looking over at her best friend in the class. "Remember, Maddie?"

Maddie just barely nodded. She hated speaking in front of other people.

"Can you tell us about what you saw, Janey or Maddie?" Mrs. Lam asked.

Janey spoke up quickly. "Um, a family went to the Brookfield Zoo in Illinois. Their little three-year-old boy was running all over the place. He was jumping on the cement steps. Swinging on the rail. He was waving his arms everywhere. The whole time he was laughing and screaming. And then, he fell. He actually fell into the gorilla area. I guess he leaned over too far. Or maybe he fell through the fence."

"He fell in?" Silas blurted out, almost embarrassed to let anyone see he cared.

"Yup! He fell like 18 feet. All the way down onto the concrete. Splat!" Janey said, scowling.

"Cool! Did he die?" questioned Silas.

"No, he didn't die, Silas. You're so gross! You always want bad things to happen. He was rescued—"

"Um-hmm," Maddie whispered. "A gorilla rescued him."

"What did you say, Maddie?" Vince asked.

"Do you guys want to know what happened or not?" Janey demanded.

"Go ahead, Janey and Maddie. Fill us in on all the details you know," said Mrs. Lam. She glanced around the room. Her eyes told each student to sit and listen politely.

"Well, like I said, the little boy was running around and goofing off," Janey continued. "I mean, he was only three years old! Anyway, he began to climb the fence. So he could see the gorillas better. It wasn't like they were doing anything exciting.

Just the mother and baby gorillas hanging out. I guess the little guy just wanted to get closer to the gorillas or something."

"And he did, didn't he? He got to see them so close—"

"Silas, please," interrupted the teacher. "Let the girls finish. This is the last time I'm going to ask you nicely. Go ahead, Janey."

"All of a sudden everyone heard a big slap. You know, it sounded like when someone does a belly flop! Then all eyes looked down below. There was the little boy lying like he was dead or something. He just lay there.

"I bet his mother was going crazy," said Janey. "I know my mom would have been.

"Then all the people began to freak out. They were screaming and calling for help."

The class listened quietly. Even Silas wasn't talking.

Janey went on. "One lady leaned really far over the edge and tried to reach the boy. It looked like she might fall too!"

"That was when someone noticed the mother gorilla moving toward the boy!" added Maddie.

"Oh yeah, she's right," Janey said. "So after the kid fell into the pit, nobody knew what to do. It looked like things were gonna get pretty ugly down there. There's the boy just kind of lying there. No one could reach him.

"And now a gorilla was walking slowly over to him. And she was huge! She probably weighed like 400 pounds. That little boy didn't weigh more than 30 pounds! She just needed to sit on him to kill him. But she didn't."

"What did she do?" asked Mrs. Lam.

"Well, she just stared down at the little boy. Then she reached her long furry arm out to him. She took hold of the boy's wrist. Then she lifted his arm and then let it fall. Like they do on murder shows, you know. And then they ask, 'Is he alive?'"

"Perhaps she was feeling for a pulse," suggested Vince.

"Uh, I don't think so, Vince," sneered Silas.

"But then," Maddie couldn't help herself from adding something. "The mama, her name is Binti Jua, picked up the little boy. She just scooped him right up. She held him the exact same way she had been holding her own baby. She hugged him close to her chest!"

"Wait a minute! You girls are crazy," Silas said. "A gorilla did not pick up the boy to help him. She picked him up to eat him!"

"No, she didn't," said Janey. "She carried him away toward the door where she gets fed. She knew people would be around there. Then she waited for someone to come and help. And they did! So now the boy is fine. And Binti Jua is a hero!"

Silence, wide eyes, and open mouths all greeted the end of Janey's story.

"Whatever!" Silas groaned.

"Do you want to add anything, Maddie?" asked the teacher.

"Um, well, yeah. When Binti was carrying the little boy, another gorilla tried to get near her. But Binti wouldn't let her. She hugged the little boy even closer to her chest."

"See. That proves it. I told you she was trying to kill him!" stated Silas.

Mrs. Lam stared hard at Silas. Then she looked toward Maddie. "Why do you think that is, Maddie?"

"Well," started the shy eighth grader, "I read in a book once that most mothers don't like others to touch their babies. Maybe Binti was kind of thinking that the little boy was like her baby. She didn't want the other gorilla to touch him."

"You're so weird, Maddie! How could a gorilla think that a kid was her baby? Was the little boy wearing a gorilla costume?" teased Silas.

"Hush, Silas! Maddie has made a very good point," commented Mrs. Lam. "Gorillas and humans have many similarities. Let's think of some."

"Ten fingers, ten toes, two ears, two eyes, a nose—"

"Thank you, Silas, you're right," interrupted Mrs. Lam. "Can anyone think of anything else? Things that humans and gorillas have that other animals don't?"

Vince raised his hand. He'd been the quietest during Maddie and Janey's story. But it was easy to tell that he had been listening very carefully.

"Vince?" Mrs. Lam called.

"Well, I'm pretty sure this happened in a different place. And I know it was a boy gorilla . . ."

"What, Vin? What happened?" Silas was much more interested now that a boy was talking.

"I don't really know precisely what happened. But I think the actual sequence of events was—"

"Whoa! Vin. Remember me? You need to talk in English. None of this big word stuff!"

"Sorry, Silas. Anyway, I think it was a little boy, just like the other time. And he fell into the pit. This time, though, he was saved by a male gorilla. Jambo was his name, I think.

"But the gorilla didn't pick up the fallen child," Vince added. "Jambo stood over the boy. So that no other gorilla could get near."

 11

"See? Even gorillas think other gorillas will eat people!" Silas blurted. "I'm not stupid, you guys! I can't believe you're buying this junk!"

"Perhaps, Silas, but I don't think so," Vince said calmly. "Anyway, Jambo waited patiently until someone came to help the boy. And he didn't budge. He was determined. No other gorilla was going to get close!"

"So, how come he didn't do what the other gorilla did?" Silas asked. "He probably just thought the kid was a toy or something. He didn't want anyone to take it."

"You know, Silas, you're kind of right," Mrs. Lam chipped in. "I saw a program on the Discovery Channel that talked about gorillas. It said that male gorillas like to guard what is theirs. They do not want to share!"

"Me neither," offered Janey. "When my little sister borrows my clothes, it drives me crazy! I hate it!"

"Yes, Janey, I'm sure," smiled Mrs. Lam. "When Jambo guarded the boy, it was kind of like you guarding what's yours.

"And female gorillas like to snuggle with what is theirs," Mrs. Lam added. "Just like mothers do. If a little boy falls, his mother cuddles him to make him feel better. Binti did the same thing with the little boy who fell into her pit.

"So that was a very good point you made, Silas," said Mrs. Lam. "See, there's another similarity between humans and gorillas."

"I think gorillas are just great big hairy people," Janey added dreamily.

"Well, I'm not sure about that, Janey! But wouldn't it be fun to find out more about them?" asked Mrs. Lam.

"Yeah, we could have Gorilla-Awareness Week," said Janey.

"That might even be fun," Silas muttered. "Do you think that maybe I could wear a gorilla costume, Mrs. Lam?"

"We'll see about that, Silas! But what do the rest of you think? Vince? Maddie? Would you like to dedicate this week to researching gorillas?"

There were low sounds of sures, okays, and yeahs.

Just as Mrs. Lam began to speak, the bell rang. It marked the end of the period. Chairs scraped along the floor. The room suddenly burst into noise.

"Just a minute, please, kids. For tomorrow, I'd like each of you to bring in one fact about gorillas—just one. See you tomorrow."

"I have something to tell right now," Janey said. "And it's kind of neat."

"Let's wait, Janey," Mrs. Lam said. "We'll all hear about it tomorrow."

"OK," Janey agreed.

"Bye, Mrs. Lam," the students called.

"Good-bye, Mrs. Lam. See you tomorrow," Vince said quietly.

"Bye, Vince."

The door closed, and Mrs. Lam was left with her thoughts.

Chapter

Koko

It was Tuesday—computer day. And it was Jess's favorite day of the week. Mrs. Lam's class usually worked on the computers the whole period.

Yesterday, Jess had spent the whole day playing on his own computer. He had been home with a 102° temperature. His mother hadn't said a thing when she'd seen how high his temperature was. It was so easy to warm up the thermometer on the radiator.

Mrs. Lam had sent home the assignment on gorillas with Jess's brother. So Jess had had a real reason to be on the computer.

As Jess rode the bus to school, he thought about the gorilla Web site. Would he be able to find out more there? He hadn't found it until last night. And then his father had forced him to turn off his computer.

When Jess reached his classroom, all of his classmates were talking to each other—even Maddie. It looked like she was holding some kind of book in her hands. And everyone was

struggling to see better. It was probably pictures of her needlepoint. Or maybe even better, her antique doll collection. Girls liked such stupid stuff!

She never talks, Jess thought to himself. So why would smart-aleck Silas bother to listen? Of course Vince would, because Vince always does whatever he's supposed to. How come people like people who always do the right thing?

Jess had promised himself he'd only hang out with the cool people. Vince wasn't exactly cool, but he was kind of funny sometimes.

"Good morning!" called out Mrs. Lam.

Jess hadn't even noticed Mrs. Lam when he walked in. "Welcome back, Jess," said Mrs. Lam. "We missed you. Now, won't you sit down?" she asked quietly.

"Oh yeah, sure. Sorry Mrs. L.," Jess said. "I was just wondering what all the other kids were looking at."

"Well, as a matter of fact, Jess, so was I," said Mrs. Lam. "Maddie, is your book something you'd like to share with the class?"

Maddie looked up. Her eyes were wide. The courage she had shown for a few moments the day before had disappeared. She was back to being the quiet girl in Mrs. Lam's class.

"Come on, Maddie," urged Janey. "Tell Mrs. Lam what you just told us."

"Yes, Maddie, please do. What you were saying earlier was absolutely fascinating!" added Vince.

Maddie looked up at Vince. His smile made her feel much better.

"I'll try," she said quietly.

"Perfect," said Mrs. Lam.

With that Maddie reached into her desk and brought out a book titled *Koko's Story*. She held it up so that everyone could see the cover. There was a funny little gorilla on the front. She had a yellow cube in her mouth. Even Jess looked up.

"Is that the gorilla that saved the kid at the zoo?" shouted Silas.

  15

"Uh...no," hesitated Maddie. "But it is her aunt. This is Koko. She's different from other gorillas. She can talk to humans."

"Oh no, not again," moaned Silas. "Now, you guys don't really buy that, do you?" he said, looking at Jess and even Vince.

"She is?" asked Janey. "Koko is Binti Jua's aunt?"

"I think that's marvelous. How did you ever find that out?" asked Mrs. Lam.

"Well, actually, it was Jess who told Vince, and Vince told me," answered Maddie.

"No, you didn't!" Silas looked at Jess. He couldn't believe Jess would ever even talk to Vince. "You told Vince?"

"Yeah, why not? When I was surfing the Net last night, I looked up gorillas. I got some info on that accident at the Brookfield Zoo. You know, the one where the little boy fell into the gorilla pit."

"Yes," said Mrs. Lam. "As a matter of fact, we discussed that yesterday. While you were gone."

"Well, it said that the gorilla at the zoo was the niece of some other famous gorilla," Jess continued. "Then I ran into Vince in one of the chat rooms—"

"You talked to Vince on the phone?" Silas asked, horrified.

"Silas, shhh, please," came from every direction.

"Give it up, Silas!" moaned Jess. "A chat room is a place on the computer, moron! Anyway, I asked Vince what he had found. He said something about a gorilla named Koko. I realized that was the name of the gorilla related to the one who rescued the boy in the zoo."

"Well-done, you two!" exclaimed Mrs. Lam. "You make quite a team! Now, Maddie, go on with all of your wonderful discoveries."

"Koko was born in the San Francisco Zoo on July fourth," Maddie began. "Her real name is Hanabi-Ko. That means 'fireworks child' in Japanese. When she was really little she got sick. She had to go to the zoo hospital. Then she got better. After that she was sent to the Children's Zoo—"

"Why?" demanded Silas. "Would the other gorillas have tried to eat her?"

Maddie didn't hear him. Or if she did, she just ignored boring old Silas.

She continued, "That was when Koko met the lady who wrote the book—Dr. Patterson. Dr. Patterson began teaching hand signs to Koko. You know, for words like food or drink. The doctor used the same signs that people who can't hear use."

  17

Helen Keller

"I know some signs," Janey offered. "I read a story about Helen Keller. I liked it so much that my parents gave me a whole book on sign language. It shows pictures of shapes you can make with your hands to show words. Then there's a chapter that shows how to make the letters with your hand. Should I bring it in?"

"That's a great idea, Janey. Does anyone else know sign language?" asked Mrs. Lam.

Silas raised his hand quietly. He hoped no one would notice.

"Yes, Silas," said Mrs. Lam. "Do you know some words in sign language?"

"Uh, well, yeah! Actually, my older sister can't hear. So my whole family knows how to sign. That's how we talk at dinner, even though Lara can read lips. Sometimes, though, my little brother and I forget to face her. And that messes everything up. So we try to sign at mealtime."

All of his classmates stared quietly in disbelief. But Mrs. Lam didn't seem at all surprised.

"Well, Silas, perhaps one day this week you could teach us some words. Would you do that for us?"

"Sure, whatever," Silas mumbled.

"Anyway, go ahead, Maddie," said the teacher.

"The doctor was teaching the baby gorilla signs. But no one could tell if Koko was understanding what was going on. Then one day Dr. Patterson was about to give her some breakfast, and Koko made the sign for food. *Food* was her first word. Since then she has learned more than 700 signs. She can even show if she's mad or sad—"

"Can she show if she's bored?" teased Jess as he pretended to snore.

Silas shot Jess a killer look. If Jess wanted to be Silas's friend, he'd just blown it. Silas was pretty interested in what Maddie was saying. (He didn't think Jess needed to be such a smart aleck.)

"Just kidding," Jess added quietly.

Maddie hadn't heard or noticed anything that Jess and Silas had said. Talking about Koko had made her more confident than ever before. She was a different girl! She had so much to say.

"Anyway, the doctor was so excited. Now she was sure Koko knew what the signs meant. Then Koko was so happy she began to run around—"

"—and act like a monkey?" Vince asked in spite of himself.

"Yeah, exactly!" Maddie said excitedly. "Day after day, the doctor and Koko played and signed. Koko learned all sorts of things. One time she even asked to be tickled by tapping her armpits!"

Everyone laughed at that—even Jess!

Maddie was on a roll. There was no stopping her now.

"Then when Koko was five, they brought another gorilla to the Children's Zoo. His name is Michael. Dr. Patterson wanted to teach another gorilla sign language. That way maybe the gorillas could sign with each other. Michael is actually the same kind of gorilla that Koko is."

"What do you mean by the same kind, Maddie?" asked Mrs. Lam.

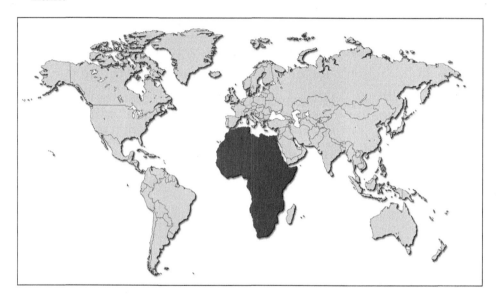

"Um, well I think there are different kinds of gorillas. And I read that Michael and Koko are from the same place in Africa. Michael was born there. And even though Koko was born here in America, her ancestors lived there. Or something like that!"

"Wow! So they're a long way from home. What if Koko and Michael still lived in Africa? I wonder how different things would be for them," said Mrs. Lam.

"I would imagine quite a bit!" said Vince. "What do you think, Maddie?"

"I guess so," Maddie answered. "I mean, the book shows how Koko's day is filled with people and lessons."

"There probably aren't too many gorillas signing in the jungle!" Silas said, half laughing.

Janey was surprised that Silas had said something nice. That didn't happen too often.

"Well, Maddie, what is Koko's day like?" Vince questioned.

Mrs. Lam looked around her class. She only had five students. But she couldn't remember the last time everyone paid attention at the same time. Today was different. Everyone was interested and involved—everyone.

Mrs. Lam looked from student to student. There was Jess, the class clown. And Janey, the class talker. She hardly ever gave anyone a chance to speak. And then Maddie, the animal lover. Vince, the polite gentleman. And Silas, the tough guy who never said anything serious. That is, until ten minutes ago when he had told everyone about his sister.

Yes! Mrs. Lam thought. We may discover just as much about each other as we do about gorillas on this little safari!

"So, Maddie, do you know what Koko does every day or not?" demanded Jess.

"Yeah. She has a regular schedule just like we do. At 8:30, she wakes up and has breakfast—cereal and fruit. Then she has to go to school. Well, she doesn't exactly go to school. But she has class time. That's when she learns more signs. Around 10:00 she gets bored. So she and Michael have recess. They get to ride tricycles and play with dolls and little stuffed or rubber animals."

"Sounds good to me," Jess muttered.

Maddie kept going. "Then it's back to work at 11:00 for more signing lessons and tests. After that, it's lunchtime. Then there's free time for the teacher to plan different projects. Around 4:30 it's time for a mostly vegetable dinner. Koko's just like me. She hates mushrooms and radishes!"

"Yuck! Me too," exclaimed Janey.

"After that, Koko has free time to play with her own toys. At 7:00 she goes to brush her teeth and get ready for bed. She likes to put off going to bed, even when she's tired."

  21

"Yeah, same with my little brother. He always has a fit when my parents say it's bedtime," Silas said.

"So, anyway, that's it. Then Koko goes to bed," Maddie finished.

"Thank you, Maddie," said Mrs. Lam. "That was absolutely wonderful. It's fun to think about a gorilla having a life not so very different from ours. How could we find out more about Koko? Has anyone heard anything?"

"I know," Jess called out. "Why don't we go online? Maybe Koko has a Web site! I mean, if there's a gorilla site, why not a Koko site?"

"That's a good idea. Can I go log on, Mrs. Lam?" Janey asked.

"Let's let Jess go. It was his idea."

Janey nodded her head. She didn't like Mrs. Lam's answer. But she knew her teacher was trying to be fair.

With that, the class left their seats. They wandered to the back of the classroom.

"You get everything ready, Jess. The rest of us will glance through the book Maddie brought in. I bet there are some adorable pictures."

"Oh, there are lots!" Janey chimed in.

As the class turned the pages, Jess typed quickly. It wasn't long before he called, "Hey! Look, you guys. Look at this. I found Koko's very own Web site! This is so cool!"

Jess looked pleased. He was smiling a real smile.

"There's something about Koko and a kitten," Jess said. "She takes care of a little kitten like it's her own baby. It says she wanted a cat after she saw some in picture books. So at Christmas, the doctor gave her a fake cat. That didn't cut it. Koko wanted a live kitten. And she got one! She looked at three pictures of cats. She chose a tailless tabby."

"My next-door neighbor has one of those. It looks just like a big fur ball!" said Maddie.

"Koko named her kitten too. She signed 'All Ball.'"

Jess looked up at Maddie and smiled. "She chose that name," he said, "because the kitten had no tail and looked kind of like a ball! Just like your neighbor's cat, Maddie."

"Now Koko is a mother!" exclaimed Janey. "She has her very own little baby to care for."

"At first, the doctor kept All Ball at her house. She worried about what Koko might do to him.

"Then one night, Ball sneaked into Koko's trailer all by himself," Jess added. "Koko never hurt Ball. And Ball knew she never would!"

"Can I see now?" asked Janey.

"Let's all take turns," suggested Vince.

Janey sat down and took over. "Koko and Ball played together all the time. Sometimes Ball got bored. Then he would just wander away. Still, Koko and Ball were the best of friends. They totally loved each other.

"Koko figured that Ball would like all the same things that she liked," Janey continued. "But Koko was wrong.

"Koko wanted Ball to tickle her. But Ball didn't want to tickle or be tickled. So Dr. Patterson and Koko pretended. The doctor held Ball in her hand while she tickled Koko. And this was good enough for Koko.

"Another time," Janey said, "Koko wanted to play blow-it. This game meant blowing as hard as she could into Ball's face. Ball wasn't too thrilled about this game, either!"

Everyone laughed at the image of a 400-pound gorilla blowing into the soft, fuzzy little face of a 4-pound kitten.

"Anyway, they were still able to have lots of fun together. But then . . . oh no!" cried Janey.

"What? What?" everyone asked. "What happened?"

"Oh no!" was all Janey could say.

"What, Janey? Tell us!" demanded Silas. "What's wrong?"

"One day," Janey began. But then she couldn't finish.

So Jess took over again. He read aloud to Mrs. Lam and his classmates. "When the doctor arrived at the zoo one day, she heard bad news. One of the workers told her that poor little Ball had been hit by a car. He was dead."

All the children stood in silence. Even Mrs. Lam was stunned. Not one of them could imagine how Koko was going to feel when she found out.

Jess continued. "When the doctor heard the news, she was really sad. She didn't know what Koko would do. But the doctor knew that she had to tell Koko right away. And she did. Dr. Patterson explained that Ball had been run over by a car. And Koko would not be able to see her again! Koko didn't do anything. So Dr. Patterson wondered if the gorilla understood. She decided to leave Koko alone for a bit."

Jess paused. But no one spoke. Then he went on. "A few minutes later, the doctor heard sad noises coming from Koko's trailer. Actually, what she heard was a 'distress call.' It's a noise all gorillas make when they are upset about something. Koko was crying over Ball.

"When Dr. Patterson asked Koko about Ball a few days afterward, Koko made the sign for cry. She was sad. Then she rubbed her hands across her eyes. This was the sign for blind. Koko was saying that she would never see Ball again. After that, whenever Koko saw a picture of a cat in one of her books, she would frown and become sad."

"I don't blame her," whispered Maddie. "I remember when my dog got hit by a car. I couldn't stop thinking about her!" Maddie's face was sad. And her voice shook as she spoke.

"Yeah," Silas said. "My sisters got all upset when our hamster ran away. They were all sad and stuff. I told them he was probably running around the house somewhere. Some morning little Squiggy will probably be sitting on the kitchen table just waiting for them."

"You guys want me to finish?" asked Jess.

"Go, go!"

"A couple of months later, Koko said she wanted another kitten. Dr. Patterson kept trying to find the right one. Once she was sure she had the right one. But it didn't work. And Koko got totally upset again.

"But finally Dr. Patterson found the right kitten to replace Ball. A little striped cat. Koko reached out and brought the kitten to her chest. She petted him gently. She wouldn't even let Dr. Patterson hold him. Koko just looked at the doctor and made the sign for baby. Koko was a Mama again!"

"That's so neat!" Janey said. "It's like Koko wanted to have a baby all her own. She knew exactly what she was supposed to do."

"Yes," Vince remarked. "She behaved just like Binti Jua at the zoo. It seems their maternal instincts—"

"Their what?" Silas asked.

"The way to be a mother comes naturally to them," Vince explained. "No one has to teach them what to do. It's like when our cat had kittens. She just wandered off into a corner. Then she had her babies all by herself. And she didn't even leave a mess. After that, she took care of them without any help. She just knew what to do."

"I wonder why Koko doesn't have any babies of her own," Maddie said.

"Maybe it says something on the computer. Does it Jess?" Vince questioned.

"Um, I'm looking. Here. It says something about needing other gorillas in the zoo so they can have babies. They don't want the gorillas to become extinct."

"Well, who's *they?*" demanded Janey.

"The people at a place called The Gorilla Foundation," answered Jess. "The same people who support Dr. Patterson. They make it possible for her to work with Koko and Michael.

"Now they've brought in another gorilla. They want this new gorilla, Ndume, and Koko to maybe have a baby. But check this out. There are all these things about each of the gorillas."

Everyone gathered around Jess's chair and stared at the screen.

26

	KOKO	MICHAEL	NDUME
Full Name	Hanabi-Ko		
Translation	Fireworks Child		Male
Hair Color	Warm to dark brown	Black with reddish hair on his head & a silver back	Black with silvering back
Eye Color	Dark brown	Light brown	Warm brown
Height	5' ¾"	Approx. 6'	Approx. 6'
Weight	280 pounds	425 pounds	360 pounds
Birthday	July 4, 1971	March 17, 1973 (unofficial)	October 10, 1981
Place of Birth	San Francisco, CA	Cameroon, Africa	Cincinnati, OH
Vocabulary	Uses over 500 signs (Knows over 1,000)	Uses over 350 signs	Uses natural gorilla gestures & vocalizations
Favorite Color	Red	Yellow	Blue
Favorite Foods	Nuts, gourmet tofu dishes, apples, corn on the cob	Nuts, apples, peanut butter sandwiches	Peanuts, carrots, apples, bananas, potatoes, celery
Favorite TV Shows	Wild Kingdom	Sesame Street Mister Rogers	Alf
Favorite Movie	Free Willy		Dinosaurs
Favorite Toys	Rubber alligators	Construction pipes	Blue 50-gallon plastic barrel, phone books, cardboard boxes
Favorite Book	The Three Little Kittens		
Favorite Activities	Playing with dolls, playing chase, drawing, writing	Listening to opera by Luciano Pavarotti, playing with sounds and rhythms, playing chase, looking at pictures	Eating, sleeping in the sun, playing chase
Family Members	Father: Bwana Mother: Jacqueline Brothers: Sunshine and Mkubwa plus nieces and nephews in zoos all over the U.S.	No known relatives	Many relatives and three offspring in zoos around the U.S.

"This is so cool. How do they know that *Free Willy* is Koko's favorite movie? I mean, is that the one she watches the most carefully or something?" questioned Silas.

"Who knows? But doesn't it make perfect sense that her favorite book is *The Three Little Kittens*?" Vince remarked.

  27

"Oh, I hope she has a baby. She loved Ball so much. And now she has her new kitten. She'd be such a great mother!" Maddie added.

"Well, it says right here that they need these gorillas to have babies. Otherwise they'll become extinct," said Jess.

"Couldn't they just go back to Africa and get more?" Silas asked.

His question was greeted with five sets of horrified eyes.

"What?" he demanded. "Well, couldn't they?"

"Where have you been, man?" Jess asked. "Gorillas are like the most precious animals in the world! People in Africa are killing them. And now there are barely any left! We have to take care of them!"

"No way, Jess. How do you know that? There will always be gorillas in Africa! Just like there will always be dogs and cats in America! You guys believe everything you hear!"

"I'm not kidding you, Silas," said Jess.

"Actually, Silas, I do think that Jess has a point," said Mrs. Lam. "However, I think the best way to find out would be if we all did a little research. How many of you were able to do last night's homework and find a fact about gorillas?"

All the children raised their hands. As far as Mrs. Lam could remember, this was a first. Somehow, for some reason, someone had always claimed to have forgotten. But not today.

"Okay. Well, how many of you found out facts about gorillas in captivity?" asked Mrs. Lam. "And how many of you found out something about gorillas in the wild?"

"Captivity."

"Captivity."

"Well, kind of both," Maddie said.

"What do you mean 'kind of both,' Maddie?" asked Mrs. Lam.

"Well, I only had actual information on Koko. But remember I talked about the kinds of gorillas? Michael and Koko are the same kind because they are from the same area in Africa. There are some other kinds too. I think there are three kinds. Koko and Michael are from western Africa. They

 28

are one kind of *lowland* gorilla. Then there are some from eastern Africa. And they are also *lowland* gorillas. And then there are *mountain* gorillas. But that's really all I know."

"Then, for tomorrow, why don't we all try to find out something about gorillas in the wild?" said Mrs. Lam.

With that, the bell rang.

"Perfect timing," Mrs. Lam said over the noise of the five students getting ready to leave. "Okay, I'll see you all tomorrow. And Maddie, a special thanks to you for your book. Jess, thank you for finding the Koko Web site."

"No prob, Mrs. Lam. See you tomorrow," Jess said, walking out the door.

"Yeah, see ya, Mrs. L.," said Silas.

"Bye, guys."

The door slammed. Everyone had left. That is, everyone but Maddie.

"Mrs. Lam," Maddie started, "did it ever make you nervous to speak in front of people?"

"You bet it did!" Mrs. Lam replied. "I still get nervous before the first day of school. I have trouble sleeping the night before. As soon as I begin to see you and your friends arrive, my stomach gets all fizzy.

"But, I'll tell you something else. The more I do it, the easier it becomes. And, most importantly, if you really want to stand up for something, you don't want your fears to get in your way!"

"I know," said Maddie. "Sometimes I hear people say really mean things that they want to do to animals. I want to say something. I really do! But then I get all nervous."

"Well, you did a *great* job today. See if you can't say some more tomorrow."

"Yeah, I'll try. I guess. Thanks," answered the shy girl.

"Thank you, Maddie! See you tomorrow," said the teacher.

"Yeah, see you tomorrow, Mrs. Lam."

Imagine, Mrs. Lam thought. A gorilla having her own "home" on a computer! What will they think of next?

Chapter 3

Wild Gorillas

Mrs. Lam arrived at school early on Wednesday morning. And she was *not* the first one there. In fact, she arrived last.

The eighth-grade teacher looked at her students. She thought about the beginning of the year. One student had been too shy to speak. One had been too bored to speak. One had spoken only out of politeness. One had spoken only when he had something disgusting to add. And one had spoken all the time without ever listening to anyone else.

Today those five kids were gone. They had been replaced by interested and involved students. Mrs. Lam watched quietly without interrupting. And she felt good about what she saw.

Maddie, Silas, Vince, Janey, and Jess sat in a circle. All eyes were on Silas as he made movements with his hands. He was signing, Mrs. Lam realized. No one had noticed Mrs. Lam's arrival.

"Good morning, everyone!" she called.

"Morning," said the class with their eyes never leaving Silas's busy hands.

"Hi, Mrs. Lam," Janey responded. "Look at Silas. He's signing what he learned about gorillas. It's really neat. This is how he and his family talk at dinner. I know my father would love that! Imagine me talking in silence! He says I talk way too much."

Everyone laughed at this.

"What's so funny?" she demanded. "Why are you looking at me that way?"

After a moment of silence, Vince spoke slowly. "It's not that you talk too much, Janey. It's just that you always have something to say. But I like it. It makes it easier for me. Then I don't feel like I have to speak as much."

Then everyone really laughed. There wasn't a head in the room that wasn't nodding in agreement.

Mrs. Lam spoke up to change the subject. "Silas, I'd love to see some of your signing. But before we do, let's see what everyone learned last night."

Silas stopped signing and everyone turned to face Mrs. Lam.

"What did you discover about gorillas in the wild?" the teacher asked.

"Well, I couldn't find out anything about lowland gorillas. You know, the kind Michael and Koko are. But I learned a lot about mountain gorillas!" said Vince.

"Me, too," said Jess.

"That's all right, boys. In fact, that's perfect! You two can tell us about them a little later. But first, did anyone find out more about the lowland gorillas?"

"Yes," answered the other three together.

"Why don't you start then, Silas?"

"Could someone else go first?"

"I'll go," Janey offered.

"Perfect, then. Why don't you start?" said Mrs. Lam.

"Well, it's just like Maddie said yesterday. There are three types of gorillas. Two kinds of lowland, the eastern and the western. And then there are mountain gorillas. I guess Vince and Jess know all about them. Anyway, their names come from where they live in Africa.

"The western gorillas are the biggest group. That's because they have the most land to live on. They live in tropical forests. That's where they can find the most food. Michael and Koko are western lowland gorillas.

  31

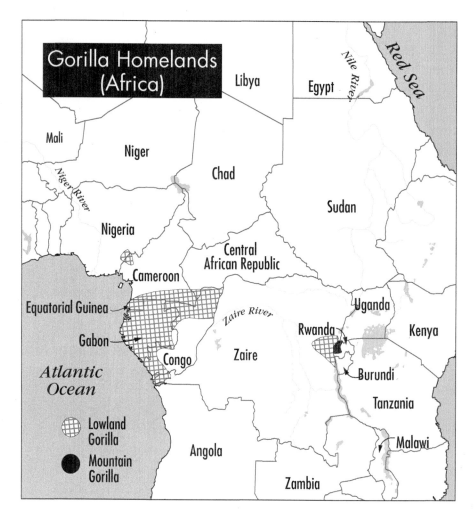

Gorilla Homelands (Africa)

Libya · Egypt · Red Sea · Nile River · Mali · Niger · Chad · Sudan · Niger River · Nigeria · Central African Republic · Cameroon · Equatorial Guinea · Zaire River · Uganda · Kenya · Gabon · Rwanda · Congo · Zaire · Burundi · Atlantic Ocean · Tanzania · Angola · Malawi · Zambia

Lowland Gorilla
Mountain Gorilla

"There are something like 20,000 of them alive," continued Janey. "Well, actually, they don't really know exactly how many are alive. Even so, there are at least 10,000 of them. And maybe even close to 40,000. It's pretty hard to tell because they live in so many different countries."

Mrs. Lam pulled down the map as Janey spoke on. "The western gorillas live mostly in Cameroon, Congo, Central African Republic, Gabon, and Zaire." The teacher pointed out the countries.

"See this big bulge on the left side of Africa," she said as she pointed at the area. "The western lowland gorillas live here. Right at the curve just below the bulge."

  32

"Then there are the eastern lowland gorillas," said Janey. "There aren't as many of them as there are of the western ones. Only about 4,000. And almost all of them are in the country of Zaire on the eastern side of Africa. My book said that only 24 of them live in captivity. Oh, and I forgot—"

"How many of the western kind live in captivity?" Silas interrupted.

"I was about to say. So shh!" Janey demanded. "There are at least 550 western gorillas in captivity. This is the kind that most zoos have. So, that's probably the kind that you guys have seen."

"That was wonderful, Janey. You found out a lot!" commented Mrs. Lam.

"Oh, but wait, I have more," Janey protested.

"Well, why don't we listen to what Silas and Maddie have to say first? But thank you, Janey, for your information. Silas or Maddie?"

Neither one of them said anything. Maddie was too shy. And Silas was too proud. Everyone waited. Silas slowly raised his hand.

"Silas?"

"Well, I guess what I learned is about all gorillas— even the mountain gorillas. Almost every gorilla is a member of a gorilla group. Each group is kind of like the others—I mean, a gorilla group is sort of like one of our families."

   33

Silas paused, but no one spoke. So he continued. "There's a head gorilla, and it's always a guy gorilla. He's called the silverback. It's because when he is about ten years old, the hair on his back begins to turn silver. Kinda cool, huh? And by the time he's 12 years old, his back is almost totally silver. His hair shows that he's older and more mature!

"He's almost like a president or something," Silas continued. "Because he makes all the decisions for his group. And he's the leader forever. No one gives him a hard time. Except maybe another silverback from a different group. Sometimes the silverback gets worried, though. He worries that another male gorilla in his group might take away some of the females."

"So then there are other gorillas who will challenge the silverback?" asked Jess.

"Well, not really, 'cause almost all the males leave by the time they're eight years old," Silas explained. "But in a lot of groups, there's one other male who stays around until he's like 13 years old! The groups have about three or four females. The females usually stay loyal to their silverback—"

"As they should," said Jess with a slight chuckle.

Silas smiled. "They stay with the one silverback unless he is their father. If so, then the female goes off to find another group. That way she is not related to any of the males or the silverback."

Maddie raised her hand slowly.

"Yes, Maddie?" answered Mrs. Lam.

"I don't think I really understand what the silverback does. It sounds kind of like the other gorillas in the group do whatever they want. My father sure doesn't let me do whatever I want. I know that!"

"It's different, Maddie," said Silas. "Gorillas don't worry about the same things that we do. There's no TV. And guess what else?" he turned his head in the other direction. "There are no telephones! What would you do, Janey?" Silas kidded.

"Oh, cut it out. I could handle that," Janey answered, laughing.

Silas continued. "The silverback is the one who leads the group on its daily adventures. He decides where, how far, and how fast the group travels. He is also the one who is supposed to protect them. But I guess once they have all done what he wants, then they can do whatever *they* choose."

"I wonder how it all works out. I think it's so neat that even though they roam around such a huge space, they are still able to find a family." Maddie said this so quietly it was almost a whisper.

"Thank you so much, Silas," said Mrs. Lam. "That was great."

Silas grinned.

"Okay, Maddie," Mrs. Lam said, turning to look at her shy student. "I think you also had some information for us about mountain gorillas."

For a moment, Maddie paused. Then her excitement won out.

"Actually, Mrs. Lam," she began, "I found out what their days are like. In the tropical forests, the gorillas wake up early in the morning. Around 6:00. After that, they eat breakfast. But they don't eat cereal and bananas like Koko. They do eat some fruit, though.

"Gorillas are kind of vegetarians," Maddie went on. "They eat leaves, branches, bark, vines, and other things that grow in the forest. But then again, they're not really vegetarians because they eat gross little bugs. They even eat termites!

"They dig them up with their fingers. And then they stick a whole bunch in their mouths. Sometimes, though, they share with one another."

"Now that's pretty cool!" Silas cheered. "My buddies on the baseball team dared our shortstop to eat a worm. We each chipped in a dollar, and gulp—Jordan swallowed that slimy worm in one big breath!"

It was easy to see that Mrs. Lam had wanted to stop him. But she didn't. She was glad that Silas was involved enough to know what they were all talking about.

"Eeeewwww," shrilled Janey. "That is so disgusting! Did he throw up afterward?"

"Nope. Once that worm went down, it stayed down. It just kept squirming and wiggling and—"

"Maddie, would you please continue?" Mrs. Lam thought Silas had added enough.

"Um, sure," answered Maddie. "Once they finish breakfast—"

"Wait, wait," called out Jess. "Do they ever drink anything?"

"Nah, they don't need to. They get all the water they need from the fruits, vegetables, and flowers they eat. Then after breakfast, guess what they do for the next four hours? They play. Then they eat some more. Then they nap. And then they just hang out! They do this because they have to rest up for their daily adventure."

The word *adventure* captured the attention of some who had gotten a little bored.

"What kind of adventure?" came from various desks.

Maddie blushed. "Well, it's not really an adventure. But this is the time when the silverback gets to be the leader. The whole group has to move to wherever the silverback decides. Sometimes they'll only move 100 yards in one direction—"

"Big deal!" cried Jess. "That's like walking from one end of a football field to another."

Maddie looked directly at Jess and continued. "And other days, they might go more than a mile. It's up to the silverback to make all the decisions. They move so they can find as much

   36

food as possible. Anyway, once they get to wherever they're going, they stop and build their nests. Their nests are beds. And then they go to sleep until the next morning. They are just like babies. They probably sleep close to 12 hours a night. Plus an hour or two during that morning nap time. I think it sounds perfect!"

"Me, too," agreed Silas. "Nothing to do but eat, play, and make sure you have a bed to sleep in. Now *that* I could handle!"

"You really think so?" questioned Vince. "I think you'd get bored. Come on, Silas, don't you think you'd miss your skateboard? TV? Pop-Tarts?"

Silas laughed. "Maybe a little, but I'd like to give it a try. How 'bout it, Mrs. L.? Maybe we should live 'a day in the life' of a gorilla. What do you think?"

"Well, you know, Silas, it's not a bad idea. But before you become so sold on becoming a gorilla living in the African lowlands, I think you should know something else about their lives. Humans haven't always been very nice to gorillas. In fact, some people used to kill them just to show off. Cutting off parts of a gorilla's body was like having a trophy. They just murdered them for fun!"

At that little piece of knowledge, Silas's eyebrows shot up.

"That's exactly what I read last night," said Vince. "There are horrible things that happen to gorillas all the time, but now—"

The passing bell rang, interrupting all of them. But no one moved. They all waited for Vince to finish what he was saying. Instead, Mrs. Lam spoke.

"Oh, Vince, I'm sorry. Everyone is so anxious to hear what you were going to say. But we'll have to wait until tomorrow.

"And Maddie, Silas, and Janey, you can tell us all the things you may have forgotten to share with us today. I must tell all of you that you've taught me so much. You're really doing a wonderful job with this project. Perhaps we should consider Silas's idea to have a gorilla day for the whole school—"

"Then I could wear a gorilla suit!" exclaimed Jess with a ridiculous smile on his face.

"I don't know. We'll talk about it!" Mrs. Lam answered. "Good-bye, class. I'll see you first thing tomorrow. You've done a great job!"

"Bye Mrs. Lam, see you tomorrow." The voices trailed off.

Chapter 4

Murder in the Mountains

On Thursday when Mrs. Lam reached her classroom, she was again the last person to arrive. Maddie, Janey, Silas, and Jess sat motionless in their seats. Vince was telling a story filled with lots of interesting and sad details.

No "good mornings" greeted Mrs. Lam. Someone said, "Hey, Mrs. L., you should hear what Vince is saying."

Someone else said, "We need to rent a movie about some lady! Whoa, this is cool!"

Mrs. Lam steered her way to the front of the room. She tried to listen as she unpacked her backpack.

"Good morning, everyone," she interrupted.

"Oh, yes. Good morning, Mrs. Lam," said Vince.

"Hey, Mrs. L.," called a few others.

"Hi," Maddie mouthed gently.

"So, Vince, what is it that your classmates find so interesting? Would you mind starting over?"

"No, not at all, Mrs. Lam. I'd be happy to."

"Start with the guys coming in and killing—," Silas began.

"Shhh, Silas! Let Vince do whatever he wants," Jess said.

"Boys!" said the teacher. "Go ahead, Vince. You start wherever you think is best."

Dian Fossey

"Okay, here goes. Imagine you're a woman in the middle of a tropical forest in Rwanda. That's a country right next to Zaire in eastern Africa. You moved from America so that you could live near these gorillas. Some people think you're completely cuckoo!

"Now, you've already been in Africa for about ten years," Vince continued. He had everyone's attention. "And you spend every day watching the gorillas! By now, the mountain gorillas don't even really notice you. Even those right on the other side of a tree don't care that you're there. They know you. They may even think that you're one of them."

"Wow! And this chick didn't even need a costume!" exclaimed Jess.

The others forced a weak laugh. But it was easy to tell they wanted to listen to Vince.

"Remember, you're in the forest," Vince went on. "And it almost looks as if the gorillas are playing tag. They probably are.

"There's a silverback pretending to chase one of the smaller males. The smaller one runs. But when the silverback is about to tackle him, the small one stops. Then he curls up in a ball.

  40

He makes a strange sound. It sounds kind of scary at first. Then you realize he's laughing—"

"Oh, yeah. That's right!" interrupted Jess. "I read that the mountain gorillas have a language all their own. A silverback will hoot when he's worried that another gorilla might be trying to tempt some of the females."

"How'd you learn that, Jess?" asked Janey.

Jess just rolled his eyes and continued. "Sometimes, though, gorillas scream when they're scared. Or they grunt at each other when they're mad. They might even bark fast in a high-pitched voice. They do that when they want to know something—when they're curious. You know, kind of like Janey," Jess added with a smile. "And best of all, when they belch, it means they are just totally happy. Kind of like . . . no, not you, Janey. Like a cat when it purrs."

"That's awesome," said Silas. "Now, if I burp at home, I'll tell my parents it's 'cause I'm just happy. What do you think?"

"I tried it last night," groaned Jess. "Didn't work too well!"

"Vince," Mrs. Lam said quietly. "Why don't you continue?"

"Okay. Um, where was I?"

"You were talking about how all the gorillas were playing tag and just having fun! It still makes me want to be one," added Maddie softly.

"Right, right!" said Vince. "Also, just a little ways away, there are two females sitting quietly with their babies. It looks like they're picking in each other's fur. Somewhere else not very far away, two of the younger males are wrestling."

"Where's the silverback?" demanded Silas.

"Good question, Si," Vince answered. "It looks like the silverback is playing with one of the other gorillas. But he isn't. He's really watching what everyone is doing. Like a baby-sitter!"

"If the silverback gets hurt or feels sort of sick, then the whole group has to wait for him to get better," Vince continued. "Remember, the silverback is the one who decides everything for the group. Anyway, when this happens, the other gorillas get bored."

"No kidding!" exclaimed Janey. She moved from sitting in her chair to on top of the desk. "I guess it's like when my mom is sick. I can't do anything! I can't go anywhere. 'Cause she's the one who drives. It stinks!"

"Yeah, well, it's not too good for the gorillas either," agreed Vince. "They want to move around. But because the silverback feels bad, all the others have to hang around. They try to have fun or do something. You know. Just like us when it rains or snows and we have to stay inside. The gorillas make up games and play while the silverback sleeps."

"What happens if one group runs into another?" asked Maddie.

Mrs. Lam smiled. "I was just about to ask that very question, Maddie."

"Usually, all the groups that roam around the same area kind of know each other," Vince explained. "And since all gorillas try to respect each other, the new group usually leaves. But even so, there's a lot of hooting and chest pounding by both silverbacks. That way they can both sort of feel powerful! It's like when I argue with my sister! She always has to have the last word. It's totally stupid!"

"Wow!" exclaimed Mrs. Lam. "That is absolutely amazing! But what's even more incredible, Vince, is that you know all this! How *do* you know this?"

Vince looked at Jess. Then they both looked at the class.

"Well," Jess began, "Vince came over to my house yesterday after school. So we could work together." Jess looked at Silas to see his reaction. But Silas was too interested in the gorillas. No one cared anymore about who was cool or who wasn't.

"Anyway," Jess continued, "on our way home from school, we stopped by the library. We found the most awesome book. It was about the wacky lady Vince told you about. You know? The one who moved from America to the jungle just so she could kind of live with the gorillas.

"Well, she lived there for 13 years," Jess said. "She went to see the gorillas every single day. It didn't matter whether

it was raining, or sunny, or what! She always went to see
them.

"She followed all the different groups that lived near her.
Then she numbered each group. She also gave a name to every
gorilla in every group. She could tell each one apart from all
the others. That way she knew if one left his group and joined
another. Or she could tell if one was missing."

"Weird," said Silas. "How could anyone tell one gorilla from
another? If you've seen one, you've seen them all."

  43

"You know, Silas. Gorillas probably think the same thing about humans. And we don't all look alike, do we?" asked Mrs. Lam.

"No way," answered Silas.

"Well, like Vince said earlier," Jess continued, "this lady watched what the gorillas did every day. She saw what happened when two groups ran into each other. She saw gorillas fight. She watched them play. She saw everything she'd hoped to see. But then one day—"

"Wait, wait, wait," cried Janey. "What's her name?"

"Dian Fossey," said Vince softly.

"Yeah, she's the one! I saw a movie about her. It was called *Gorillas in the Mist*. And she—"

Mrs. Lam held up her hand. "Just a second, Janey. Let's let Jess and Vince finish."

"Janey's right, Mrs. L.," said Jess. "That must be the name of the movie. 'Cause that's the name of the book that Vince and I checked out of the library!"

"Yes, yes!" agreed Mrs. Lam. "But I wanted the two of you to be the ones to tell us about the mountain gorillas. Janey had her turn yesterday."

"You want to go, Vince?" Jess asked.

"Sure!" Vince agreed. "Anyway, one day when Ms. Fossey was out watching, she saw that one of her gorillas had been hurt. His leg had gotten caught in a trap. It was totally broken. Well, after asking some people questions, she found out that poachers—"

"Who?" asked Silas.

"People who kill animals even though it's against the law," explained Vince. "They do it so they can make money off the animals. Poachers would kill the gorillas and sell their hands as ashtrays. Or they'd just take the heads and sell them. Sometimes, though, they wouldn't even kill them. They'd kidnap them and sell them to zoos or private owners."

Mrs. Lam looked around her classroom. Everyone stared in silence. Maddie didn't even blink.

"Are you all right, Maddie?" asked Mrs. Lam.

Maddie turned her head slowly. "Does this still happen?"

"Um, well, Dian Fossey did her very best to make sure that it wouldn't happen. At first, she messed up any of the traps that had been set—"

"She did this *all* by herself?" asked Silas.

"Well, no," began Vince. "After she had been in Rwanda for a while, she set up a research station in the Virunga Mountains. Actually, they're not mountains. They're really volcanoes!

"Anyway, she had a whole bunch of houses built. Lots of different kinds of people went to work there. Some were from England. And some were from Africa. But everyone who went was there to study the gorillas or to help protect them.

"The gorillas were really in trouble," Vince continued. "People were trying to kill them or steal them.

"In 1981, there were only like 250 mountain gorillas left in this area—and maybe the whole world. Then people all over the world began to hear about the really horrible things that were happening. A foundation was set up called the Mountain Gorilla Foundation."

"The foundation has its own Web site. Just like Koko does," offered Jess.

"Perhaps we could find out a bit more about that foundation for tomorrow," suggested Mrs. Lam.

"Or maybe we could have a bake sale to raise money," Maddie said. Then she looked around, worried that she had said something stupid. But her classmates were nodding their heads.

"That's a good idea, Maddie," said Janey.

"Yes, let's talk about some other ideas like that tomorrow. Think about what we can do to help Dian Fossey and her gorillas," said Mrs. Lam.

"But Mrs. Lam. There's more. A lot of people liked what Dian Fossey was doing because it was helping the gorillas. But there were others who hated her."

"Yeah, I bet," said Janey. "Like the mean guys who were hurting the gorillas. You know? The poachers."

Dian Fossey

"Yeah!" said Jess. "And they got even more angry when she began to arrest the poachers herself if she found them. Sometimes she'd tie them up. She'd make them wait until she could take them into town. Then once they got there, they'd have to go to jail!

"Dian Fossey really went after the poachers. Because of her, they got into lots of trouble if they even tried to *hurt* the gorillas."

"Good for her!" cheered Janey.

"Yeah, what she was doing was good for the gorillas," agreed Jess. "But a lot of people, even some who liked her ideas, thought she was going kind of crazy. It was like she was obsessed or something."

"Well, it pretty much sounds like she was," said Silas. "She cared more about the gorillas than the people."

 46

"Y-Yeah," stuttered Maddie. "But the humans were bad. Everything they were doing was mean! They were hurting the gorillas. And the gorillas weren't even doing anything!"

"Anyway," Jess jumped in, "something really weird happened. It was two days after Christmas in 1985. Some of Dian Fossey's friends went up to visit her. When they got there, they found her dead in her cabin. Someone had broken in and killed her. But no one knows who did it. Not even now."

"Oh, my gosh," came from everyone's mouths. "They killed her?"

"Yep! And she was buried in the gorilla cemetery. It was where she had buried all the gorillas who had died or been killed. I guess like two-thirds of all the gorillas who died had been killed by poachers!"

"I can't believe she died," said Janey. "How do they know she was murdered and didn't just die all by herself?"

"Well," started Vince, "her house was all torn apart, and . . . her head was, well, like pretty much split in half. There was blood all over her face. She couldn't have done that to herself."

"Eeeewww," shrieked Janey.

"So then what happened?" Mrs. Lam asked. "Has anyone continued Ms. Fossey's work?"

Vince answered. "Well, like I said, she had done a lot before she died. She had people go out and patrol for poachers. That was a big help!"

"And she started raising money. She made where the gorillas lived places for tourists," added Jess. "That way, people would pay money to see her gorillas. She always called them hers. That made people really think she was wacko!

"Anyway, it's really expensive to go on one of these trips," Jess continued. "But people went and still go."

Vince spoke up again. "But more than that, she let people know what was happening—people around her and people all over the world. She made the gorillas real. Even for us who live so far away from them. She told the world."

"Does that mean that people are still working to protect the gorillas?" asked Maddie. "Even though Dian Fossey is dead?"

"Yep," Vince assured her. "And that's not all. They're still studying the gorillas. It's sad, though, because there's another problem. The gorillas live right in between two countries that are at war. It got so bad that the people at the research station had to evacuate in 1994. Then in 1995, seven gorillas were killed by poachers! That proves that when no one's around, the poachers take over."

"That's awful," moaned Maddie.

"But there's good news. In January of 1996, there were nine more gorillas."

"Well, now that is exciting! Maybe we should—," began Mrs. Lam.

The bell broke into her sentence. But not one of the children moved.

Mrs. Lam addressed her waiting students. "Why don't we all come in tomorrow with ideas of how we, as students at Samuel Taylor Middle School, might be able to help. Also, let's talk about Gorilla-Awareness Week," suggested Mrs. Lam.

"Okay," said Janey. "But what about Silas? Can he still teach us to sign?"

"Yeah!" everyone said.

Silas just shrugged his shoulders.

"Well, Silas?" asked Mrs. Lam.

"Sure, Mrs. Lam, I can do that."

Slowly, the students of Mrs. Lam's eighth-grade class made their way to the door.

"See you tomorrow," they called.

"See you tomorrow," Mrs. Lam answered.

Tomorrow would be the last day of this wonderful week. Oh, how Mrs. Lam hoped her students had learned as much as she had. What would tomorrow be like? she wondered.

48

Chapter 5

Save the Gorilla

It was Friday. The end of the week. But it didn't feel like it.

Mrs. Lam walked to her classroom. She couldn't wait to tell her students what she had discussed with the principal.

Marching into her classroom, Mrs. Lam began talking right away. But then she stopped. She looked around. The classroom was empty. And there were no approaching sounds in the hallway.

Slowly, Mrs. Lam sank down into her desk chair. What had happened? She had thought that, for once, her eighth graders were excited about class. But even the gorillas in Africa, Koko in California, and Binti Jua in Illinois couldn't make these eighth graders want to come to school. Mrs. Lam just wanted to cry.

Then the door to the classroom opened slowly.

"Morning, Mrs. Lam," a voice said.

"Morning, Vince," the teacher said. She didn't even look up.

"Where's everyone else?" Vince asked.

"Oh, I don't know," Mrs. Lam moaned, slowly raising her head. A rustle at the door caused her to turn her head. Her eyes opened in absolute wonder. There in the doorway were all of her students. But they weren't alone. A man was standing next to Maddie. And he was holding a little bundle of soft brown fur.

"Mrs. Lam," said Maddie, "this is Dr. Hans Gardner. And this," Maddie said, pointing at the furry little creature, "is Bongo. She's two years old. She was born at the zoo."

"H-h-hello, Dr. Gardner," stammered Mrs. Lam. "And hello to you, Bongo. Welcome to our class!"

"Thank you for allowing us to come. This is Bongo's first visit to a school. She seems a bit shy right now."

"Would someone like to explain?" Mrs. Lam asked, looking puzzled. She was shocked to hear Maddie speak up.

"Um, well, I was telling my mother about everything we'd learned during Gorilla Week. And she got an idea. She ran to the phone and dialed—"

Just at that moment, Bongo jumped out of Dr. Gardner's arms. Then she leaped onto a desk. She jumped from one desk to the next. It looked like she was playing dot-to-dot.

The whole classroom burst into life. The students scattered as Dr. Gardner quietly called to the galloping baby gorilla.

Bongo seemed to have her own idea of what to do. At first, she kept bouncing around and running into things. But then she slowed down. Everyone stopped where they were and just watched. Even Dr. Gardner. They all watched as Bongo headed straight for Silas.

Silas was signing.

"Look!" Janey whispered. "Bongo knows how to sign!"

Dr. Gardner laughed. "You're right, young lady. And so does your friend. Where did you learn that?"

"My sister's hearing-impaired," Silas offered. "She taught me."

"Well, that's wonderful. Bongo and I were going to save that for the end. But now you've seen it. How did you know to sign?"

"I really didn't," Silas muttered, "but I thought I'd try. I mean, those gorillas in California, you know—"

"Yeah, Michael and Koko," Janey jumped in.

"Janey!" Mrs. Lam motioned for her to let Silas talk. "Go ahead, Silas."

"Anyway, yeah, Michael and Koko. We've been studying gorillas. We learned that they sign. So I figured maybe your gorilla could too."

"Oh, she's not my gorilla," said Dr. Gardner. "While it may be the zoo who pays for her, she really belongs to herself. We must be careful about believing that we ever own animals. What else have you learned?" asked Dr. Gardner.

Five hands shot up. Mrs. Lam was suddenly reminded why she had been so excited to come to school today. She had been right. Her eighth graders did want to be here.

"Jess?"

"We learned that there are gorillas who live in the lowlands of Africa. They're called eastern and western. And there are also mountain gorillas."

"Vince?"

"We read about a smart woman who gave her life to study the gorillas—"

"Yeah, and she got murdered," added Silas.

"We learned that there is a war right where the gorillas live. And all their land is getting taken over by people," added Janey.

Maddie said something, but no one could hear.

"Yes, Maddie, what did you say?" asked Mrs. Lam.

Maddie sat up straight in her chair.

"Worst of all," she said loudly, "we learned that there are people called poachers who kill gorillas. They're horrible!"

"You're right, Maddie," said Dr. Gardner. "Poachers are awful."

"But what can we do about them?" cried Janey.

"Well, someone said that you studied a lady in Africa. Was that Dian Fossey?" the doctor asked.

A chorus of "yes" greeted his question.

"Perhaps you also learned that she did her best to get rid of the poachers. This was a very important step."

"Yeah, but aren't the poachers the ones who killed her?" asked Silas.

"Oh, I don't think anyone knows for sure. But we do know they didn't like her very much. However, she also did some other things to help the gorillas."

"I remember," offered Jess. Mrs. Lam looked at Jess and smiled.

"I do. I swear," Jess assured everyone. "Dian Fossey made it so that people would pay to see the gorillas. That way there would be money for people to stay in Africa and keep studying the gorillas. She also tried to tell people about the gorillas. She probably figured the same way as Mrs. L. You guys know what I'm talking about! What does Mrs. L. always say?"

"Knowledge is power," four voices said.

"I bet that's what Dian Fossey thought too!" Jess added.

"Well-done, Jess!" exclaimed Mrs. Lam.

Jess smiled.

"You're right, Jess!" added Dr. Gardner.

"Well, that's all great," said Janey. "But what are we gonna

do? I mean, gorillas are still being killed. And that lady is dead. Who's going to take care of them?"

"Some people still live at the research station in Rwanda," said Dr. Gardner. "They returned after the evacuation. They're doing the best they can."

"But that's not enough!" Janey insisted. "We need to do something here!"

"Speaking of here," said Vince. "I saw something last night when I was surfing the Web. It was about Koko. You know, the gorilla who signs words. The people at the foundation are trying to raise enough money so that she and Michael can go to Maui. There is a huge chunk of land there that they could live on."

"Maui!" exclaimed Silas. "You mean like Hawaii? That is so cool! I heard that place has some of the biggest waves in the world. I'm telling you, those gorillas will have it made!"

"They don't surf, moron!" declared Janey.

Silas shot her an ugly look.

"Anyway," continued Vince, "they chose Maui because it's the most like Africa. There's a lot of forest. Then Michael and Koko could kind of live a life like the gorillas in Africa."

"And there wouldn't be any poachers, either," Maddie added.

"Nope. Not one!" said Vince. "I also read that most of the zoos have agreed not to buy any gorillas captured from the wild. That way the poachers won't want to kill or kidnap any more gorillas."

"That's all very true," interrupted Dr. Gardner. "But the biggest threat to gorillas is losing their homes. Wars, more people being born, and more people needing homes. All of these take away from the gorillas. So the thing that's helping the gorillas the most is the money from visiting tourists. But there's still more to do. Lots more."

"Well," said Mrs. Lam. "I have an idea. It won't help the gorillas right away. But it is one of the things that Dian Fossey thought we should do."

"I bet you don't want us to go out and undo traps!" Jess said, laughing.

   53

"No."

"Or visit Africa and pay to see the gorillas?" suggested Janey, smiling.

"Nope."

"You want us to make sure that other people find out about gorillas, right?" asked Maddie softly.

"Exactly, Maddie! And I know just how we're going to do it!" said Mrs. Lam.

"How? How?" voices cried.

"Now, everyone sit down. Even you, Bongo," the teacher said.

At the sound of her name, the little gorilla looked up. She waddled her little body over toward the teacher. And in one leap, she was sitting on Mrs. Lam's lap.

"That wasn't exactly what I meant," laughed the teacher. "Oh well!"

Everyone laughed.

Mrs. Lam continued. "I spoke with the principal about having an all-school Gorilla-Awareness Week. He thought it was a wonderful idea. He said we can have assemblies each day with information and skits. Silas can teach sign language. The whole school can learn about gorillas in zoos and in the wild. Just like we have."

"Then we could try to raise money," offered Maddie. "We could send it to that foundation in California. We could get other people to become members of the foundation. And then they would raise money. And they would get more members." Maddie's voice rose in excitement. "And best of all, we could give the world knowledge."

"And what is knowledge?" asked Mrs. Lam.

"Knowledge is power!" said her eighth graders.

The bell rang to mark the end of class. No one made a move or a sound. Then Bongo began to clap her hands together.

The world certainly needs gorillas! And the more the better!

For More Information

If you are interested in contacting The Gorilla Foundation, you may do so by mail, email, or telephone.

THE GORILLA FOUNDATION
P.O. BOX 620-6530
WOODSIDE, CA 94062-9901
TEL: 1-800-63-GO-APE
WEB SITE: www.gorilla.org

James Jacobson at the Gorilla Foundation, writer of the newsletter at the Koko Web Site:
EMAIL: hanabiko@earthlink.net

Or, if you are interested in finding out information on Koko:
WEB SITE: http.//www.koko.org

Or, if you are interested in sending email to Koko:
EMAIL: koko@poboxes.com

Index

Africa, 20, 28–29, 31–33, 40, 45, 51, 52, 53, 54
    Cameroon, 27, 32
    Central African Republic, 32
    Congo, 32
    Gabon, 32
    Rwanda, 32, 40, 45, 53
    Virunga Mountains, 45
    Zaire, 32, 33, 40
All Ball, 23–25
Binti Jua, 7–11, 13, 16, 25, 49
Brookfield Zoo, 8, 17
Children's Zoo, 17, 20
Fossey, Dian, 42–48, 51–53
The Gorilla Foundation, 26, 53, 54, 55
gorillas
    eastern lowland, 29, 31, 33, 51
    female, 11, 12–13, 34, 41
    male, 11–12, 34, 40–41
    mountain, 29, 40, 44–45, 51
    western lowland, 29, 31–33, 51
Gorillas in the Mist, 44
Hanabi-Ko, 17, 27
Jambo, 11–12
Koko, 15–29, 31, 49, 50–51, 53, 55
Koko's Story, 15
Michael, 20, 21, 26, 27, 28, 31, 50–51, 53
Mountain Gorilla Foundation, 45
Ndume, 26, 27
Patterson, Dr., 17–20, 22–26
poachers, 44–48, 51–53
San Francisco Zoo, 17
sign language, 17–21, 50
silverback, 34–36, 40–42